I0820787

ANIMAL ALBUMS
THE DOG FAMILY
BY ALEX MONROE
eureka!
UREKA!, AN IMPRINT OF BELLWETHER MEDIA BY FLUTTERBEE

Eureka! books turn real stories into unforgettable experiences. Clear, direct language and sharp, captivating imagery make it easy to follow your curiosity, one fascinating fact at a time.
Your Eureka! moment awaits!

For information regarding permission, write to Bellwether Media, Inc., Attention: Permissions Department, 3500 American Blvd W, Suite 150, Bloomington, MN 55431.

Library of Congress Cataloging-in-Publication Data is available at www.loc.gov or upon request from the publisher.

ISBN: 9798893048568 (hardcover)
ISBN: 9798893049565 (ebook)

Editor: Rebecca Sabelko Designer: Josh Brink Series Designer: Jeff Kollock

Printed in the United States of America, North Mankato, MN.

TABLE OF CONTENTS

WHAT ARE CANIDS?

The dog family, *Canidae*, includes more than 30 species of mammals. They are often called canids. Canids live on every continent except Antarctica. They are one of the most widespread animal families on Earth! Wolves, coyotes, foxes, and jackals are all wild canids. Domestic dogs live with or near people. There are more than 340 breeds of domestic dogs.

DOMESTIC DOG

GRAY WOLVES

Most canids have strong jaws with 42 teeth designed for tearing meat. Many canid species are omnivores that mostly eat meat.

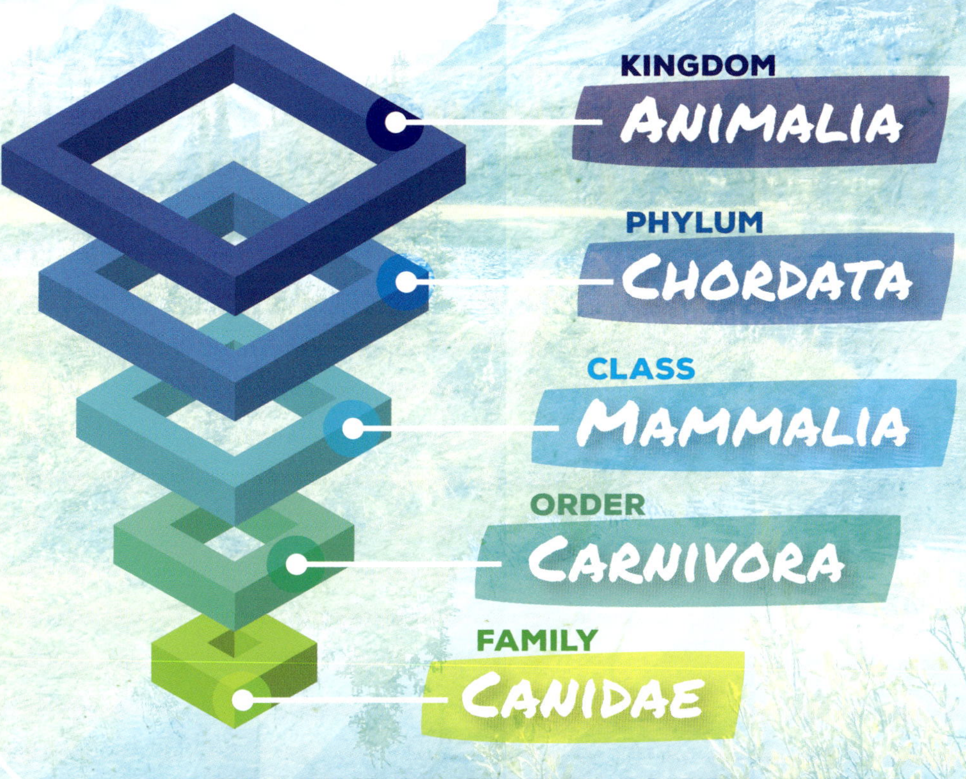

TAXONOMY CHART

JACKAL ▲

LEAVING ANTARCTICA

Explorers and scientists once used domestic dogs to carry supplies in Antarctica. But dogs have been banned there since 1994. People became worried the animals could attack and spread diseases to native wildlife.

THE HISTORY OF
CANIDS

Fossils show that the first canids appeared around 40 million years ago in North America. As Earth changed over millions of years, canids spread around the world. They also evolved and adapted to survive and hunt in new habitats. All canids developed advanced senses of hearing and smell. Larger canids, especially those that live in packs, evolved to chase prey over long distances without tiring.

FOSSIL BONES
extinct dire wolf

BREED GROUPS

The American Kennel Club puts domestic dogs into seven groups. They include the sporting, herding, hound, terrier, working, toy, and non-sporting groups. Breed standards describe the ideal traits of each breed.

GRAY WOLF

Scientists believe dogs have been domesticated for at least 14,000 years. Over time, people bred dogs to have certain appearances, personalities, and skills.

EVOLUTIONARY EXCELLENCE

LIFE CYCLE

Most wild canids form pair bonds that mate for life. They have one litter of pups or kits per year. Some species, such as African wild dogs, can have up to 20 pups in a litter! Domestic dogs that are not sterilized are often bred. They usually have one litter of puppies per year.

COYOTES

RHODESIAN RIDGEBACK LITTER

AFRICAN WILD DOG PUP

Canid pups are born unable to see or hear. Their parents care for them and keep them safe. Mothers feed their pups milk. Pups grow quickly! They learn survival skills by playing with their littermates. They also learn by watching their parents. Most canids reach adulthood when they are one to two years old.

HUSKY PUPPIES

AVERAGE LITTER SIZE

GRAY WOLF

5 PUPS

ARCTIC FOX

11 KITS

DINGO

5 PUPS

POODLE

7 PUPPIES

CANID LANGUAGE AND BEHAVIOR

SOUNDS

Canids bark, whine, scream, and growl to communicate. These sounds have different meanings from one species to another. Domestic dogs bark for many reasons, such as to show excitement or pain, but many foxes only bark when threatened.

DOG BARKING

GRAY WOLVES fighting

BODY LANGUAGE

Canids use their tails, ears, faces, and body positions to show their feelings. Most canids have relaxed bodies with lowered tails when happy. Stiff bodies with raised ears and tails show anger. Canids also stare and show their teeth.

RETRIEVER
scent marking territory

WOLF PACK

SCENT MARKING

Canids use body fluids such as urine and feces to mark territory and show they are ready to mate. In some species, scent markings define social rank.

AFRICAN WILD DOG
scent marking territory

GROUP BONDS

Canid species have varied group bonds. Some, such as wolves and dholes, live in packs. Others, like many fox species, form pair bonds. Maned wolves form territorial pair bonds.

CANID FAMILY TREE

WOLVES ▲
3 species
A gray wolf's howl can be heard up to 10 miles (16 kilometers) away.

COYOTES ▲

▲ JACKALS
3 species
Fossils show that black-backed jackals are one of the oldest canid species.

▲ DINGOES

▲ DOMESTIC DOGS
more than 340 breeds

CANIDAE

FOXES ▲
12 species

▲ AFRICAN WILD DOGS

▲ MANED WOLVES

Maned wolves are the world's tallest wild canids. They stand about 3 feet (1 meter) tall at the shoulder.

▲ ARCTIC FOXES

Arctic foxes often use the same dens for many generations. Some have been used for 300 years!

MORE THAN 8 OTHER SPECIES OF CANIDS

CANID BIOGRAPHIES
WOLVES

Wolves are the largest wild canids. The three species are gray wolves, red wolves, and Ethiopian wolves. There are nearly 40 subspecies of gray wolves.

APPEARANCE

Wolves have furry coats that can be white, gray, brown, or black. They have long, bushy tails.

VULNERABLE SPECIES

THREATS

- habitat loss
- past predator control programs

CONSERVATION EFFORTS

- addressing habitat loss
- increasing the population through breeding programs
- reintroducing red wolves into the wild

WHERE DO THEY LIVE?

Most wolf populations are found in Asia, Europe, and North America. Ethiopian wolves live in Ethiopia, Africa. Wolves live in many habitats, including deserts, forests, tundra, and more.

DIET

Most wolves are pack hunters. They work together to take down deer, elk, moose, and bison. They also eat small mammals, birds, and fish. Ethiopian wolves hunt alone. They mostly eat rodents.

GRAY WOLF POPULATIONS

Nearly two million gray wolves once lived throughout North America. But hunting in the late 1800s and early 1900s greatly cut their numbers. Today, their numbers are growing as different programs work to rebuild their population.

SIZE COMPARISON

175LBS (79 kg)

gray wolf

50LBS (23 kg)

coyote

31LBS (14 kg)

red fox

COYOTES

Coyotes are also called prairie wolves and brush wolves. They are known for their ability to adapt to almost any habitat.

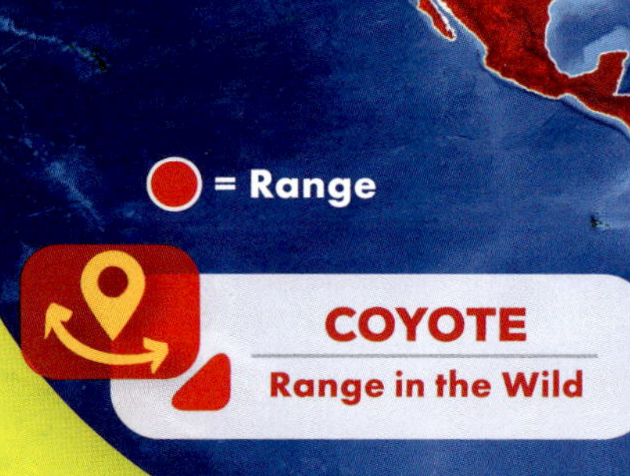

WHERE DO THEY LIVE?

Coyotes live throughout much of North America. They are found in forests, plains, deserts, and mountains. Some have even adapted to living in cities.

DIET

Coyotes hunt alone, in pairs, or in small groups. They are opportunistic feeders that eat whatever they can find. Their diet includes rodents, insects, birds, and fruit.

ON THE RUN

Coyotes can reach speeds of up to 43 miles (69 kilometers) per hour. Unlike other canids, coyotes run with their tails pointed down.

APPEARANCE

Most coyotes have grayish-brown coats. But some are black, red, or white. They have long snouts and large, pointed ears.

COYOTE SUBSPECIES

EASTERN COYOTES

- **Range:**
  northeastern U.S. and southeastern Canada

- **Known for:**
  Eastern coyotes are believed to be a mix of coyotes, wolves, and domestic dogs. They are larger than other coyote subspecies. They are sometimes called coywolves.

SIZE COMPARISON

175 LBS (79 kg)	50 LBS (23 kg)	80 LBS (36 kg)
gray wolf	coyote	Labrador retriever

FOXES

There are 12 species of foxes. The most common and widespread species is the red fox.

GRAY FOX

APPEARANCE

Foxes have small, slender bodies and long, bushy tails. Their triangular heads have long, narrow muzzles. Most species have solid coat colors.

RED FOX

DIET

Foxes hunt mostly at night. They prey on mice, birds, insects, and lizards. Foxes also eat fruit, carrion, and even garbage.

MOUSE HUNT

In open areas, red foxes can hear a mouse squeak from as far as 150 feet (46 meters) away!

WHERE DO THEY LIVE?

Foxes have native ranges throughout much of the northern hemisphere. They were introduced for sport in Australia. Foxes live in many different habitats, including grasslands, forests, mountains, and even cities.

= Range

RED FOX
Range in the Wild

ARCTIC FOX

- **Range:**
  northern Africa and the Arabian Peninsula of West Asia

- **Known for:**
  Fennec foxes are the smallest fox species. They have adapted to life in deserts. Their fur matches the desert sand. Fur on the bottoms of their paws allows them to run across hot sand. Their huge ears release heat from their bodies.

SIZE COMPARISON

31LBS (14 kg)

red fox

50LBS (23 kg)

coyote

6LBS (3 kg)

Chihuahua

JACKALS

There are three species of jackals. They are known for their loud, high-pitched howling!

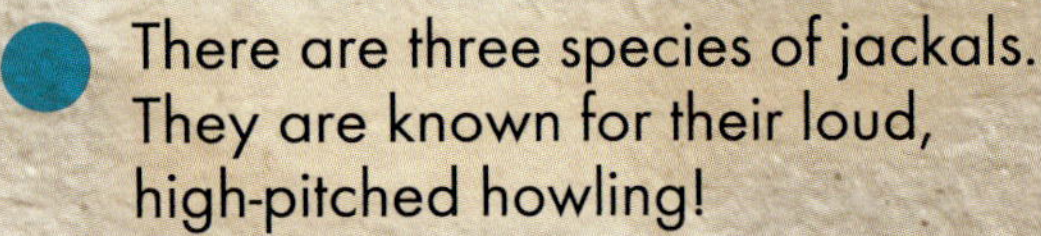

IT'S A HOOT

Side-striped jackals are known for making an owllike hooting sound. The Karamajong people of Africa named the animals "o loo" for this sound.

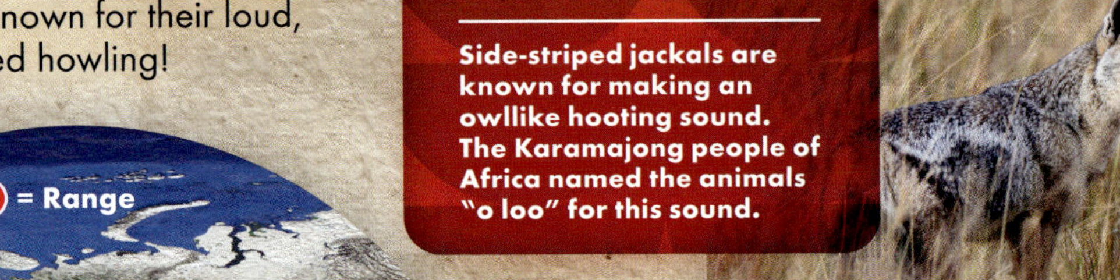

= Range

GOLDEN JACKAL

Range in the Wild

WHERE DO THEY LIVE?

Jackals live in parts of Africa, Asia, and Europe. They prefer dry plains. Side-striped jackals also live in woodlands, swamps, and mountains.

DIET

Jackals are opportunistic feeders that eat fruit, insects, and small animals. Some hunt in pairs to take down antelopes and gazelles.

APPEARANCE

All jackals have large, pointed ears and long legs. Golden jackals have mostly golden fur. Black-backed jackals are named for the black fur along their backs. Side-striped jackals have a white stripe on the sides of their bodies.

▲ GOLDEN JACKAL

THE JACKAL GOD

ANUBIS

- **Where:** Egypt
- **When:** 6000 BCE to 1782 BCE
- **Known for:** Anubis is one of the oldest Egyptian gods. Ancient Egyptians viewed him as the god of the afterlife and the guardian of the dead. He is often shown with the body of a man and the head of a black jackal-like dog.

SIZE COMPARISON

gray wolf	golden jackal	red fox
175 LBS (79 kg)	24 LBS (11 kg)	31 LBS (14 kg)

DINGOES

Dingoes are Australia's largest mammals that are carnivores.

DIET

Dingoes mainly hunt alone at night. They eat small mammals, birds, and reptiles. Sometimes they hunt in pairs or groups to take down large prey such as kangaroos. Dingoes may attack sheep and calves on ranches.

SIZE COMPARISON

43 LBS (19 kg)	24 LBS (11 kg)	80 LBS (36 kg)

dingo	golden jackal	Labrador retriever

WHERE DO THEY LIVE?

Dingoes live across much of Australia. They roam forests, plains, mountains, and deserts. Small populations live in parts of Southeast Asia.

DINGO DENS

- **Location:** hollow logs, caves, old wombat burrows
- **How long dens are used:** Dingoes use dens for about eight weeks to care for their newborn pups. Both parents care for pups. Other pack members help with care too.

APPEARANCE

Dingoes have short, soft hair and white-tipped tails. Most have golden coats, but they can also be white, yellow, or black. They have long snouts, pointed ears, and long legs. Dingoes have particularly flexible necks, wrists, and hips.

AFRICAN WILD DOGS

African wild dogs are highly social canids. Their teamwork makes them one of Africa's most successful predators!

SIZE COMPARISON

79LBS (36 kg)	43LBS (19 kg)	175LBS (79 kg)

African wild dog	dingo	gray wolf

VULNERABLE SPECIES

▼ ENDANGERED ▼

THREATS

habitat loss

diseases

hunting

CONSERVATION EFFORTS ▼

creating protected areas

educating local communities

APPEARANCE

Each African wild dog has a unique coat pattern made up of red, black, brown, white, and yellow fur. They have large, rounded ears; long legs; and bushy, white-tipped tails.

DIET

African wild dogs hunt in groups of up to 40. They often prey on antelope, but they can take down wildebeests. They also eat rodents and birds.

WHERE DO THEY LIVE?

African wild dogs mostly live in open plains and woodlands in sub-Saharan Africa.

MANED WOLF

Maned wolves are South America's largest canids. Their urine has a strong smell. It smells like skunks!

WHERE DO THEY LIVE?

Maned wolves are found throughout central and eastern South America. They live in forests, grasslands, and wetlands.

DIET

Maned wolves eat fruits and vegetables, especially lobeira fruit. They also eat small mammals and insects. They sometimes tap their feet on the ground to draw out hidden prey. Then they pounce!

SIZE COMPARISON

50 LBS (23 kg)	24 LBS (11 kg)	79 LBS (36 kg)
maned wolf	golden jackal	African wild dog

APPEARANCE

These canids are known for their long black legs that help them move through and see over tall grasses. They have thick red fur, black manes, and tall ears.

FAMOUS MANED WOLVES

MANED WOLVES OF SANTUÁRIO DO CARAÇA

- **Location:** Brazil 
- **Famous for:** Since the 1980s, monks at the Santuário do Caraça have left out trays of meat for maned wolves to eat. The tradition has helped educate people about protecting maned wolves and their habitats.

SPORTING DOGS

The American Kennel Club (AKC) created the sporting group to highlight breeds with superior hunting skills. Today, there are 33 sporting breeds. Spaniels, pointers, retrievers, and setters are the four types.

SPECIAL SKILLS

Spaniels specialize in flushing water birds into the air. Pointers and setters find game. They point with their noses. They may also set, or crouch, in the direction of game. Retrievers fetch fallen game and gently bring it to hunters.

LABRADOR RETRIEVER

GERMAN WIREHAIRED POINTER

ENGLISH COCKER SPANIEL

SIZE COMPARISON

85LBS (39 kg)

Clumber spaniel

34LBS (15 kg)

English cocker spaniel

70LBS (32 kg)

German shorthaired pointer

= Origin

POINTER

BREED PROFILE

GOLDEN RETRIEVERS

Golden retrievers are popular as both hunting companions and family dogs. They often serve as search and rescue dogs and as guides for people who are blind.

- **Size:**

75 LBS **(34 kg)**

- **Traits:**

friendly, playful, gentle, intelligent, eager to please

SHARED TRAITS

Sporting dogs sniff for game with their well-developed sense of smell. These smart dogs learn and follow commands easily. Their high energy makes them ideal hunting partners.

VIZSLA

HOUNDS

IRISH WOLFHOUND

Hound breeds were developed for hunting. Today, 32 breeds make up two main types of hounds. They are sight hounds and scent hounds.

SPECIAL SKILLS

Sight hounds use sharp vision to spot game. Some can see animals up to 0.5 miles (0.8 kilometers) away! Sight hounds can run fast. Scent hounds track game using smell, even across water. Many scent hounds have long ears that move scents toward their noses. Short legs allow them to easily sniff the ground.

SIZE COMPARISON

32LBS (14.5 kg)

dachshund

120LBS (54 kg)

Irish wolfhound

70LBS (32 kg)

greyhound

GREYHOUND

WORLD'S FASTEST!

Greyhounds are the world's fastest dogs. They can run up to 45 miles (72 kilometers) per hour!

RHODESIAN RIDGEBACK

Origin Map: Rhodesia, now known as Zimbabwe

= Origin

BLOODHOUND

BEAGLE

BREED PROFILE

RHODESIAN RIDGEBACKS

Rhodesian Ridgebacks reach speeds up to 30 miles (48 kilometers) per hour. They are famous for their history of tracking lions across African plains.

- **Size:** 85 LBS (38.5 kg)
- **Traits:** strong-willed, independent, loyal, protective, loving

SHARED TRAITS

The hound group is diverse, and most breeds make loyal pets. Their curious and independent natures aid in their hunting skills.

TERRIERS

Terriers were developed to hunt pests. The AKC recognizes 31 terrier breeds today. Breeds are further grouped as short-legged, long-legged, or bull-type.

AIREDALE TERRIER

WEST HIGHLAND WHITE TERRIER
Origin Map: Scotland

NORFOLK TERRIER

DOG FIGHTING

People once watched dog fights. But most countries outlawed dogfighting in the 1900s.

BULL TERRIER

SHARED TRAITS

Terriers are known as tough, fearless, and sometimes stubborn dogs. But they are also friendly and affectionate with people. They need a lot of exercise and space to play.

BREED PROFILE

West Highland White Terriers

West Highland white terriers were developed more than 300 years ago. Their white coats made them easy for hunters to follow. Westies hunted rodents, foxes, and badgers in packs, chasing them across rough ground.

Size:

20 LBS (9 kg)

Traits:

alert, confident, friendly, intelligent

SPECIAL SKILLS

Terriers are alert dogs that are built to dig. Short-legged terriers were bred to chase rats and other small pests underground. They tend to bark loudly and often. Long-legged terriers are fast and agile. They dig pests out from underground. Bull-type terriers were once bred for fighting. Today, they are friendly pets.

RUSSELL TERRIER

SIZE COMPARISON

70 LBS (32 kg)

Airedale terrier

12 LBS (5.4 kg)

Norfolk terrier

70 LBS (32 kg)

bull terrier

WORKING DOGS

Dogs in the working group were bred to guard property, pull heavy loads, or perform water rescues. There are currently 32 breeds in the AKC's working group.

NEWFOUNDLAND

SPECIAL SKILLS

Working dogs' large sizes help them get jobs done. Guard dogs are alert and protective. Sled and draft dogs are strong and energetic. Water rescue dogs are strong swimmers that follow commands well.

GREAT DANE

MASTIFF

WORKING GIANTS

Many of the giants of the dog world are part of the working group. Mastiffs weigh up to 230 pounds (104 kilograms)! Other large working dogs include Great Danes, Saint Bernards, and Leonbergers.

SHARED TRAITS

Working dogs are loyal pets. Many are intelligent, easy to train, and hardworking. Some dogs continue to carry out traditional jobs. Others are skilled service dogs or therapy dogs due to their strength and gentle nature.

BREED PROFILE

Siberian Huskies

The Chukchi people of northeastern Asia bred Siberian huskies to be sled dogs. In 1925, dozens of people suffered from a deadly sickness in Nome, Alaska. A sled team of Siberian huskies braved blizzards to bring them life-saving medicine.

- **Size:** 60 LBS (27 kg)
- **Traits:** smart, friendly, energetic, gentle, playful, loud

SIZE COMPARISON

45 LBS (20 kg)

German pinscher

175 LBS (79 kg)

Great Dane

80 LBS (36 kg)

boxer

HERDING DOGS

The AKC created the herding group in 1983. Before then, herding breeds were in the working group. Today, the group has 33 breeds.

GERMAN SHEPHERD

BEAUCERON

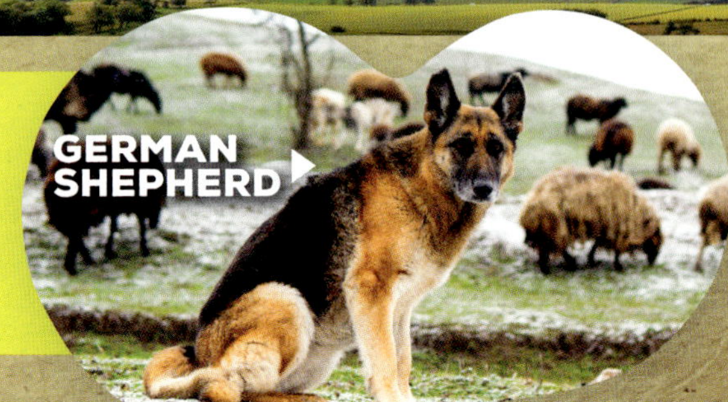

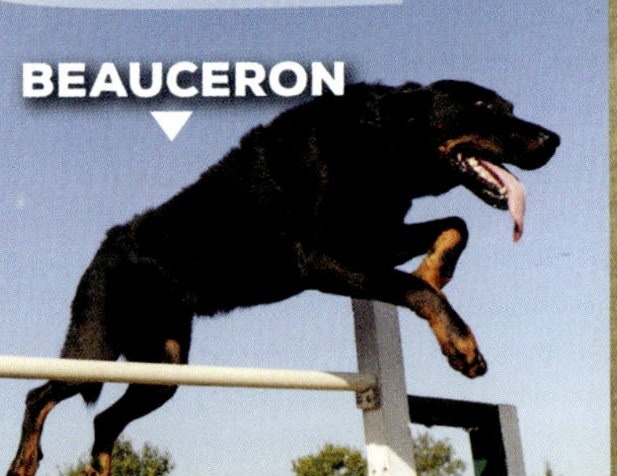

SHARED TRAITS

Herding breeds are some of the smartest of all dog breeds. These strong and athletic dogs are also agile and loyal. Their traits make some breeds ideal for police and search and rescue work. Herding dogs often succeed in dog sports.

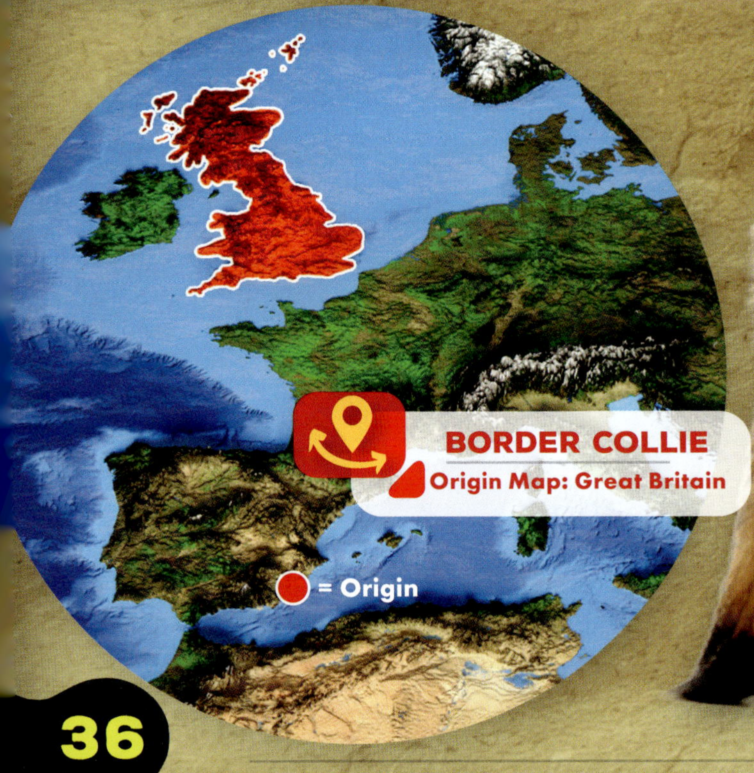
BORDER COLLIE
Origin Map: Great Britain
= Origin

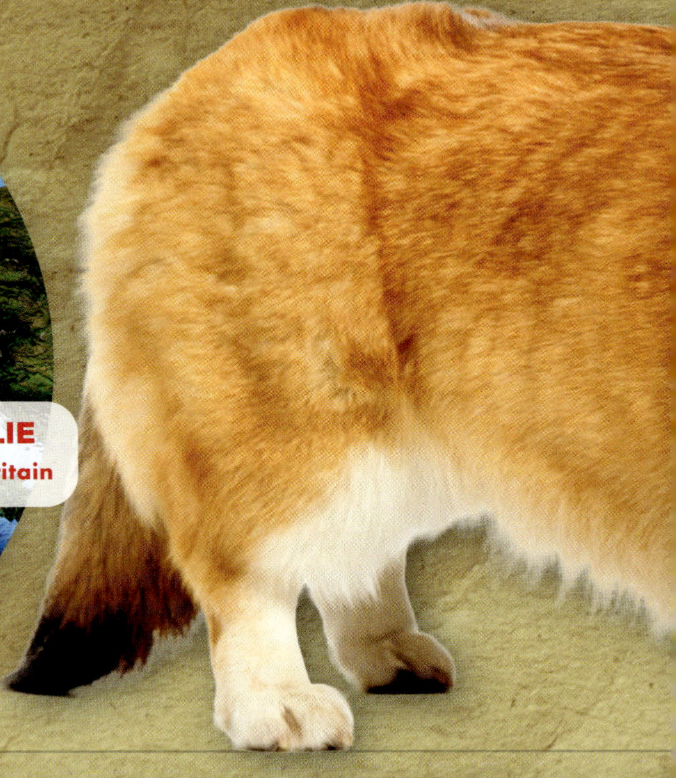

TRAINING TO SERVE

Every year, about 50 to 90 Belgian Malinois puppies are born at Joint Base San Antonio in San Antonio, Texas. The 341st Training Squadron's puppy program trains the dogs for military service to help detect explosives and track enemies.

BELGIAN MALINOIS PUPPIES

PEMBROKE WELSH CORGI

BREED PROFILE

BORDER COLLIES

Border collies were bred to be sheepherders. They can make herding decisions on their own. Border collies often win sporting contests.

- **Size:** 55 LBS (25 kg)
- **Traits:** alert, energetic, friendly, eager to please

SPECIAL SKILLS

All herding breeds have the instinct to control how other animals move. Most do not do herding work today. They often use their instincts to herd their human family members.

SIZE COMPARISON

110 LBS (50 kg)

Beauceron

30 LBS (14 kg)

Pembroke Welsh corgi

90 LBS (41 kg)

German shepherd

TOY DOGS

Toy dogs were originally bred to be pets. Dogs in this group are often small but have big personalities. There are currently 23 toy breeds.

MALTESE ▶

CHIHUAHUA ▼

SPECIAL SKILLS

Toy dogs form close bonds with their humans. Some breeds still have instincts to alert their owners of potential danger. Overall, toy dogs are mostly happy snuggling in laps and following their humans around.

SHARED TRAITS

As companions, toy dogs have bright personalities and are loyal and loving pets. Many breeds are smart and able to easily learn tricks. They make ideal therapy dogs that provide comfort and warmth.

CAVALIER KING CHARLES SPANIEL PUPPY ▶

ITALIAN GREYHOUND

SIZE COMPARISON

14LBS (6.3 kg)	7LBS (3 kg)	18LBS (8 kg)

Italian greyhound	Yorkshire terrier	Cavalier King Charles spaniel

BREED PROFILE

CHIHUAHUAS

Chihuahuas are named for the Mexican state where they were made popular in the mid-1800s. There are long-haired and short-haired Chihuahuas. Chihuahuas are one of the smallest dog breeds in the world.

- **Size:**

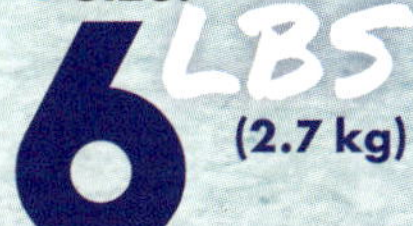

(2.7 kg)

- **Traits:**
  energetic, vocal, loyal, affectionate

NON-SPORTING DOGS

The non-sporting group is the most diverse of the AKC's groups. The AKC currently recognizes 20 non-sporting breeds.

BICHON FRISE

= Origin

FRENCH BULLDOG

Origin Map: Paris, France

SHARED TRAITS

Non-sporting breeds vary greatly in size, shape, coats, and more. Members of this group can serve as guard dogs, family pets, or both. Most are affectionate and loyal.

XOLOITZCUINTLI

CHOW CHOW

SIZE COMPARISON

70LBS (32 kg)

Dalmatian

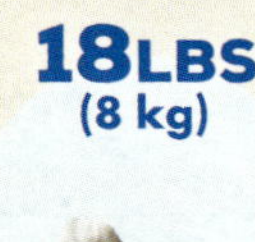
18LBS (8 kg)

bichon frise

55LBS (25 kg)

Xoloitzcuintli

SPECIAL SKILLS

Non-sporting dogs have many skills that vary by breed. For example, bichons frises' small size and fluffy coats make them adored lapdogs. Poodles are highly intelligent and easy to train as service dogs. Dalmatians' agility and energy help them in sporting events.

POODLE

DALMATIAN

BREED PROFILE

FRENCH BULLDOGS

French bulldogs are one of the most popular small dogs in the world. They are most recognized by their large "bat ears" that stand tall. Frenchies are often quiet. But they are alert watchdogs.

- **Size:**

28 LBS (13 kg)

- **Traits:**

playful, smart, adaptable, affectionate

CANIDS AND PEOPLE

Dogs have held great importance to humans throughout history. They first helped people hunt and provided safety. Over time, they became special parts of many cultures. Today, some domestic dogs continue their historic roles, while others work as service dogs to help people with disabilities. Some work with police or do search and rescue. But most are kept as loving pets.

While domestic dogs are not at risk, some wild canid species are vulnerable or endangered. They face habitat loss from agriculture, construction, and climate change that harms their homes and food sources. Humans continue to hunt some species.

MIXED BREEDS AND MUTTS

Many domestic dogs are bred from two or more breeds to create mixed breeds. Popular mixed breeds include goldendoodles, cockapoos, and cavachons. Mutts are dogs of mixed, often unknown, breeds.

Many people and organizations work to keep domestic dogs safe and healthy. Humane societies and other animal rescue programs find homes for unhoused dogs. Veterinarians encourage pet owners to sterilize and vaccinate their dogs.

Organizations around the world also help protect wild canids. Some work to save habitats while others educate people about the important roles canids have in their food chains. There are also programs that help populations grow and reintroduce species into the wild.

VETERINARIAN

DOG RESCUE SHELTER

RED FOX RESCUE

People can help wild canids by learning about them and living sustainably. Making sure predators such as canids have healthy populations helps keep Earth healthy!

GLOSSARY

adapted—changed over a period of time

agile—fast and graceful

breeds—types of domestic dogs

carrion—the rotting meat of a dead animal

climate change—a human-caused process in which Earth's average weather changes over a long period of time

cultures—societies that hold the same beliefs, arts, and ways of life

diverse—made up of animals that are different from one another

domestic—related to living near or around human settlements

draft—related to an animal that is used to haul or pull something

endangered—at risk of becoming extinct

evolved—changed from one form into a new form

habitats—natural homes of plants and animals

hemisphere—a half of the earth

instinct—a natural desire to do something

mammals—warm-blooded animals that have backbones and feed their young milk

omnivores—animals that eat both meat and plants

opportunistic—feeding on whatever food is available

pair bonds—relationships formed between two animals, usually between one male and one female

snouts—the noses and mouths of some animals

species—groups of living things that are alike and can reproduce with one another; subspecies are particular types of animals that exist within a species.

sterilized—prevented the ability to reproduce

sustainably—in a way that can be maintained at a certain rate or level

therapy dogs—dogs trained to provide comfort and support to people

tundra—a flat, treeless area where the ground is always frozen

vulnerable—at risk of becoming endangered

WRITE ABOUT IT!

- What species of canid would you like to learn more about? **Why?**
- Do you have a favorite domestic dog breed? **What** is it and **why?**
- **What** changes can you make in your life that could help keep dogs and wild canids safe?

ALSO CHECK OUT

INDEX

The images in this book are reproduced through the courtesy of: Ondrej Prosicky, front cover (African wild dog); Eric Isselée, front cover (Saint Bernard), p. 38 (skills); Florin, front cover (gray wolf), pp. 14-15 (gray wolf); mariait, front cover (maned wolf); Eric Isselee, front cover (red fox), pp. 8 (pup), 26-27; DESCHAMPS GILLES, front cover (field); JTP Photography, p. 3 (top); Harry Collins, p. 3 (bottom); BIGANDT.COM, pp. 4 (domestic), 38 (top); Geoffrey Kuchera, p. 4 (wolves); Holger T.K., p. 4 (teeth); mzphoto11, p. 5 (jackal); Historical/ Contributor/ Getty Images, p. 5 (Antarctica); Danny Ye, p. 6 (fossil); Adree1985, p. 6 (breeds); Willy Mobilo, p. 6 (wolf); Shahfahd, p. 7 (muzzle); Capture Wave Media, p. 7 (ears); Danita Delimont, pp. 7 (teeth), 19 (left); Holly Kuchera, p. 8 (coyotes); olgagorovenko, p. 8 (litter); Vova Shevchuk, p. 9 (husky); JohnPitcher, p. 9 (gray wolf); giedriius, pp. 9 (Arctic fox), 43 (top); CraigRJD, p. 9 (dingo); Олеся Болтенкова, p. 9 (poodle); Milan, pp. 10 (barking), 13 (foxes), 37 (feature); geoffkuchera, p. 10 (wolves); Fymm, p. 10 (beagle); ShaziaPhotoGhrapher, pp. 10 (language), 44 (bottom); Karoline Thalhofer, p. 11 (retriever); Raphael Rivest, p. 11 (pack); Kathy Kay, p. 11 (African wild dog); Reise-und Naturfoto, p. 12 (wolves); John Yunker, p. 12 (coyotes); knelson20, p. 12 (jackals); susan flashman, p. 12 (dingoes); ksuksa, p. 12 (domestic); ondrejprosicky, pp. 13 (African wild dogs), 24 (threats); zanna_, p. 13 (maned wolves); Menno Schaefer, p. 13 (Arctic foxes); lucaar, p. 14 (Ethiopian); Aline, p. 14 (threats); Michal Ninger, p. 14 (Arctic fox); Xaver Klaussner, p. 15; Mark, p. 16 (top); Dennis Laughlin, p. 16 (middle); outdoorsman, p. 16 (bottom); Jim Cumming, p. 17 (top); michel, p. 17 (feature); kojihirano, p. 17 (appearance); Stăn, p. 18 (top); Josh Myers, pp. 18-19; Valeriy Kirsanov, p. 18 (bottom); JoannaPerchaluk, p. 19 (middle); Hana, p. 19 (feature); Colin Stephenson, p. 20 (top); Jurgens, p. 20 (middle); Priyank, p. 20 (left); kubikactive, p. 20 (right); Stock, p. 21 (appearance); Tobie Oosthuizen, p. 21 (middle); Metropolitan Museum of Art/ Wikimedia, p. 21 (feature); Christian Musat, p. 22 (top); Jean-Paul Ferrero/ Mary Evans Picture Library/ Pantheon/ SuperStock, p. 22 (left); Harry, p. 22 (bottom); electra, pp. 22-23; Susan Flashman, p. 23 (bottom); Vincent_Nguyen, p. 23 (feature); Roger de la Harpe, p. 24 (top); Udo Kieslich, p. 24 (middle); Johannes, p. 24 (bottom); slowmotiongli, p. 25 (left); GoodFocused, p. 25 (appearance); Jerome, p. 26 (top); Evaldo Resende/ Wikimedia, p. 26 (middle); M. Skorna, p. 26 (bottom); Pedro, p. 27 (top); Pedro Carrilho, p. 27 (middle); hakoar, p. 27 (bottom); Steve Oehlenschlager, p. 28 (left); Ty Sullivan, p. 28 (middle); liramaigums, p. 29 (top); Tanya, p. 29 (feature); Nataliya Kuznetsova, p. 29 (bottom); Louis-Paul Photo, pp. 30 (top), 33 (feature); Erik Lam, pp. 30-31; LDC, p. 30 (bottom); Igor Normann, p. 31 (middle); Osetrik, p. 31 (feature); Mikkel Bigandt, p. 31 (bottom); PROMA1, p. 32 (top); robbinsbox, p. 32 (middle); alberto, p. 32 (bottom); Sandra Huber, p. 33 (skills); massininja, p. 34 (top); adogslifephoto, pp. 34 (skills), 41 (skills); Ricant Images, p. 34 (bottom); sir_j, p. 35 (feature); sommthink, p. 35 (middle); Rita Kochmarjova, p. 35 (bottom); Vitaly Zubrytsky, p. 36 (top); cynoclub, p. 36 (left); LIGHTFIELD STUDIOS, pp. 36-37; Denis Tabler, p. 37 (middle); Todor Rusinov, p. 38 (bottom); BJP7images, p. 39 (top); ArtushFoto, p. 39 (middle); otsphoto, p. 39 (feature); Anastasiia, p. 39 (bottom); Chris, p. 40 (top); niknikp, p. 40 (middle); deviddo, p. 40 (bottom); ivanastar, p. 41 (top); homydesign, p. 41 (feature); New Africa, p. 42 (service); riocontribae, p. 42 (police); julia_siomuha, p. 42 (herding); AlikeYou, p. 42 (Bottom); Bob Hogenkamp/ Wirestock Creators, p. 43 (middle); Mary Swift, p. 43 (bottom); Friends Stock, p. 44 (vet); mladenbalinovac, p. 44 (shelter); Anadolu/ Contributor/ Getty Images, p. 44 (rescue); Frank Augstein/ AP Images, p. 45 (top); Nick N A, p. 45 (middle); Cheryl Jayaratne, p. 45 (bottom left); 12photography, p. 45 (bottom middle); Sergey Demo SVDPhoto, p. 45 (bottom right).